Irish Cookbook

Traditional Irish Recipes Made Easy

iii

Table of Contents

Introduction

Thank you for choosing this book, *'Irish Cookbook: Traditional Irish Recipes Made Easy.'*

Most people believe that Irish food comprises only of mutton and potatoes. They do not know how wrong they are. The cooking techniques and food of Ireland were influenced by the rich culture and heritage of the Irish people. Irish food draws its ingredients from the available land, sea, pasturelands and moors in Ireland. Family and home play a rich role in Ireland. If you happened to pass by an Irish family's house, you will find that they all cook together in the kitchen and enjoy a hearty meal at the dining table.

History of Irish food

Irish food has been influenced by many cultures over the centuries, right from the Celts who inhabited Ireland between 600 and 500 BC and the English and the Vikings who settled in Ireland between the 16th and 17th centuries. Before potato was introduced to the Irish in the 16th century, meat was an important ingredient used in their food. This meat was often consumed only by the rich while the poor only consumed milk, cheese, butter and offal, which were complemented with barley and grains to add some nourishment.

Potato – A Blessing and a Curse

Potatoes were introduced in Ireland in the 16th century since Ireland was the perfect place to grow potatoes. The cool and damp climate allowed every family to grow potatoes in their home garden. This vegetable moved from being a garden

1

vegetable to a staple crop in Ireland for both human beings and animals since it was easy and cheap to cultivate potatoes. The Irish realized that they were able to grow potatoes even in the smallest patch in their garden.

Since potatoes are rich in minerals and vitamins, the poor consumed it in large quantities. They no longer had to depend on grains to obtain nutrition. This dependence on potatoes led to the Potato Famine in Ireland. The first time there was a famine was in the year 1739 when the weather was too cold to cultivate the crop. This episode did not have a significant impact on the Irish. However, the famine between 1845 and 1849, caused by a disease that rapidly wiped out all potato crops, led to the death of 1,000,000 Irish. Some Irish who survived either emigrated to the UK or US, while the others were left behind.

However, potatoes still remain a basic food item at every meal in Ireland. Potatoes are cooked with their skins intact. The skin is only removed at the table. The Irish believe that cooking the potatoes with their skin ensures that more nutrients remain in the potato.

Food in Ireland Today

Most cities in Ireland have a modern food culture and house multiple fast-food chains and ethnic restaurants. Some of the younger chefs in Ireland have embraced their heritage and culture and work with traditional Irish recipes. However, outside these cities, traditional Irish recipes are passed down from one generation to the next and families everywhere across Ireland cherish these recipes.

Meat

The Irish domesticated pigs for decades and maybe even centuries. This meat appears in multiple traditional Irish recipes either as sausages, bacon or gammon. Bacon and sausages and potatoes, of course, are commonly used ingredients in Irish cooking. The Irish also cook with beef and every household on St. Patrick's Day will have corned beef or Gaelic steak at its table.

Seafood and Fish

Ireland has many rivers and lakes and is surrounded by the sea. Therefore, seafood and dishes containing it play an important part in Irish cooking. Crab, oysters, lobster, cockles, white fish, fresh, smoked salmon and mussels are found easily and enjoyed by every family.

If you are intrigued by Irish cuisine, you have picked up the right book. This book covers some of the best Irish recipes, both modern and traditional, that will blow your mind. The directions given under each recipe will help you make the best version of an Irish meal.

Thanks again for purchasing this book. I hope you enjoy it!

Chapter One: Irish Baking Recipes

Irish Whiskey and Stout Chocolate Cake

Makes: 1 small cake

Ingredients:

For stout chocolate cake:

- ½ cup stout beer
- ¼ cup cocoa powder, unsweetened
- 1 large egg
- ½ teaspoon pure vanilla extract
- ½ teaspoon baking soda
- ¾ teaspoon baking powder
- 1/8 teaspoon fine sea salt
- 5 tablespoons unsalted butter
- 1 cup granulated sugar
- 6 tablespoons nonfat plain yogurt
- 1 cup + 2 tablespoons all-purpose flour

For whisky simple syrup:

- 2 tablespoons sugar
- 2 tablespoons water
- 2 tablespoons Irish whiskey

For whiskey cream frosting:

- 6 tablespoons unsalted butter, softened
- 1 cup powdered sugar, sifted
- ½ tablespoon caramel sauce (optional)
- ½ pound cream cheese
- 1 ½ tablespoons brown sugar, packed
- 1 ½ tablespoons Irish whiskey

For chocolate glaze:

- 2 ounce dark chocolate, chopped
- 1 tablespoon light corn syrup
- ½ tablespoon unsalted butter
- ¼ cup heavy cream

Method:

1. To make stout chocolate cake: Grease 2 small cake pans (of about 4-5 inches diameter) with a little butter. Place parchment paper in the pans.
2. Add beer and butter into a saucepan. Place the saucepan over medium heat. When the butter melts, turn off the heat and add sugar and cocoa and mix until sugar is dissolved completely.
3. Add egg and beat until well combined. Add vanilla and stir.
4. Add flour, baking soda, baking powder and salt into another bowl and stir.
5. Add a little of this mixture and a little yogurt into the butter mixture. Mix well.
6. Repeat the previous step until all of the flour mixture and yogurt is added.
7. Pour the batter equally among the cake pans.
8. Bake in a preheated oven at 350° F for about 35-40 minutes or a toothpick, when inserted in the center, comes out clean.
9. Cool for a few minutes in the pan before unmolding. Place on a wire rack to cool completely.
10. Meanwhile, make the whiskey simple syrup as follows: Add water and sugar into a small pan. Place the pan over medium heat and stir. When sugar

dissolves completely, turn off the heat. Cool completely.

11. Transfer into a small bowl. Chill until use.
12. To make whiskey cream cheese frosting: Fit the stand mixer with a paddle attachment. Add cream cheese into the mixing bowl and beat until creamy.
13. Add butter and beat until well combined.
14. Set the mixer on low speed and add in the brown sugar and powdered sugar.
15. Stir in the whisky and caramel and mix until well combined.
16. To make chocolate glaze: Add chocolate, corn syrup and butter into a bowl. Set aside.
17. Add heavy cream into a saucepan. Place the saucepan over medium heat.
18. When the cream begins to boil, turn off the heat and pour into the bowl of chocolate. Place a sheet of plastic wrap over the bowl to cover it. Do not stir or move the bowl for 2 minutes.
19. Stir until smooth. Do not stir or move the bowl for 2 minutes.
20. To assemble the cake: Cut each cake horizontally in the center of the cake. You will be left with 4 pieces of cake (This is a layered cake).
21. Place one layer of the cake on a cake stand.
22. Mix together simple syrup and whiskey in a bowl.
23. Brush the simple syrup mixture over the cake.
24. Spread about ¼ of the frosting (about 3-4 tablespoons) over the cake. Spread it with a leveler or a long serrated knife.
25. Place the next layer of cake.
26. Follow steps 22-25 until all the cake is used (you should be left with some frosting for the side). Crumb coat the topmost layer of the cake with frosting.

27. Chill for 15 minutes. Spread remaining frosting on the sides of the cake.
28. Chill for 10-15 minutes.
29. Pour chocolate glaze on top. Do not disturb the glaze and allow it to drip on its own.
30. Chill until use.
31. Slice and serve.

Spiced Apple Tart

Serves: 2-3

Ingredients:

- 4 ounces cream flour
- 1 ounce Irish butter
- ½ pound cooking apples, peeled, cored, cut into thick slices
- ½ teaspoon ground mixed spice
- A pinch of salt
- 1 ounce lard
- 1 ounce Demerara sugar

Method:

1. Pass flour and salt through a strainer into a bowl. Add Irish butter and lard and rub it into the mixture.
2. Pour enough cold water to make stiff dough.
3. Dust your countertop with a little flour. Place the dough on it and roll with a rolling pin.
4. Use half of the rolled dough and place in a small pie plate. Press it onto the bottom as well as the sides of the pie plate.
5. Meanwhile, add apples into a bowl. Sprinkle sugar and mixed spices over the apples. Toss well. Spread it in the pie plate over the dough. Sprinkle a tablespoon of water over the apples.
6. Cover the pie with remaining half of the rolled dough. Press both the edges of the rounds together. Make a couple of cuts on the cover.
7. Bake in a preheated oven at 350° F for about 25-30 minutes or golden brown in color.
8. Serve hot, warm or cold.

Cornflakes and Oat Cookies

Serves: 24-25

Ingredients:

- 2 large eggs
- 9.2 ounces brown sugar
- 8.5 ounces butter, softened
- 3.5 ounces sugar
- 9.2 ounces plain flour
- 3.5 ounces corn flakes
- 7 ounces oats
- 10.5 ounces chocolate chips
- 3.5 ounces dried cranberries or raisins (optional)
- 1 teaspoon baking powder
- 2 teaspoons baking soda
- 4 teaspoons vanilla extract

Method:

1. Add eggs, brown sugar, butter, sugar and vanilla into a large mixing bowl. Set the electric mixer on medium -high speed and beat until creamy.
2. Add flour, oats, salt, baking powder and baking soda into a bowl and stir.
3. Add into the bowl of eggs. Set the electric mixer on low speed and beat until just incorporated. Do not overbeat.
4. Stir in the chips, cranberries and cornflakes and continue beating on low speed until just incorporated. Do not overbeat.
5. Divide the mixture into 24-25 portions and shape into balls. Place on a plate. Press a few chocolate chips on the cookies if desired. Cover the plate with plastic wrap. Chill for 2 hours.

6. Grease a baking sheet with cooking spray. Place the cookie balls on the baking sheet.
7. Bake in a preheated oven at 350° F for about 10-12 minutes.

Irish Barmbrack

Serves: 24

Ingredients:

- 5 cups chopped dried mixed fruit
- 5 cups flour
- 1 teaspoon ground nutmeg
- 2 eggs
- ½ cup lemon marmalade
- 3 cups hot brewed tea
- 2 teaspoons ground cinnamon
- 1 teaspoon baking soda
- 3 cups sugar
- 2 teaspoons orange zest, grated

Method:

1. Grease a large Bundt pan or 2 smaller Bundt pans with a little oil or butter. Set aside.
2. Place dried fruit into a bowl. Pour hot tea over it. Cover and set aside for 2 hours.
3. Drain off the tea. Squeeze the dried fruit lightly.
4. Add flour, nutmeg, cinnamon and baking soda into a bowl and stir.
5. Add eggs, marmalade and sugar into a mixing bowl. Beat with an electric mixer until sugar is dissolved. Add marmalade, soaked dried fruit and orange zest and stir.
6. Add flour and fold gently until just incorporated. Spoon the batter into the prepared pan.
7. Bake in a preheated oven at 350° F for about 60 minutes. To check if the cake is ready: When you press the top of the cake lightly, it should spring back.
8. Cool completely in the pan. Slice and serve.

Chapter Two: Irish Breakfast Recipes

Cheesy Hash Browns

Serves: 2

- 1 onion, chopped
- 2 potatoes, grated
- Irish cheddar cheese, grated
- 1 tablespoon oil

Method:

1. Place a large frying pan over medium heat.
2. Add oil. When the oil is heated, add potato and stir.
3. Add cheese and stir. Cook until cheese melts.
4. Divide into plates and serve.

Irish Eggs

Serves: 2

Ingredients:

- 1 tablespoon butter
- 1 small onion, minced
- 3 eggs, beaten
- 3 potatoes, peeled, sliced
- ½ green bell pepper, chopped

Method:

1. Place a skillet over medium heat. Add butter. When butter melts, add onion, potatoes and green pepper.
2. Cook until potatoes are brown.
3. Add eggs and cook until the eggs are cooked as the way you like it cooked.

Rhubarb Jam

Serves: 16

Ingredients:

- 1 ¼ pounds fresh rhubarb, chopped
- 1 teaspoon orange zest, grated
- ¼ cup water
- 1 cup white sugar
- 3 tablespoons orange juice

Method:

1. Add all the ingredients into a saucepan. Place the saucepan over medium low heat. Cook until thick. Stir occasionally. Cool for some time.
2. Sterilize canning jars and pour jam into jars. Fasten the lid.
3. Refrigerate until use.
4. Use with bread slices, muffins, etc.

Irish Toast

Serves: 3

Ingredients:

- ½ loaf French bread (8 ounces), cut into 6 slices
- ½ ounce Irish whiskey
- ½ teaspoon vanilla extract
- Confectioners' sugar to dust
- 2 large eggs
- ¾ ounce Irish cream liqueur
- 2 tablespoons butter + extra melted butter to brush

Method:

1. Add eggs, whisky, vanilla and cream liqueur into a bowl and whisk well.
2. Place a nonstick skillet over medium heat. Add a little of the butter. Let the butter melt.
3. Dip a slice of bread into the egg mixture and shake off excess egg. Place bread in the pan. Place 1-2 more slices of bread in the similar manner.
4. Cook until the underside is golden brown. Flip sides and cook the other side until golden brown.
5. Repeat steps 2-4 to make the remaining toasts.
6. Drizzle some melted butter over the toasts. Brush it evenly over the toasts. Dust with confectioners' sugar and serve.

Irish Bubble and Squeak

Serves: 8 (2 patties each)

Ingredients:

- 6 cups mashed potatoes
- 2 large eggs, beaten
- ¼ teaspoon freshly grated nutmeg (optional)
- All-purpose flour, as required, for dredging
- 8 cups cabbage, shredded cooked
- 2 cups cheddar cheese, grated
- Salt to taste
- Freshly ground pepper to taste
- Vegetable oil, as required, to fry

Method:

1. Add potatoes, cabbage, cheese, eggs, salt, pepper and nutmeg into a bowl and mix well.
2. Divide the mixture into 16 equal portions and shape into patties.
3. Place in the refrigerator for 60-70 minutes.
4. Place a small deep pan over medium heat. Add oil up to half. Let the oil heat.
5. Coat the patties with flour on both the sides by dredging in the flour.
6. When the oil is heated to 365° F fry the patties in batches until golden brown and crisp on the outside.
7. Remove with a slotted spoon and place over plates lined with paper towels.
8. Serve hot.

Corned Beef Hash

Serves: 2-3

Ingredients:

- 1 ½ tablespoons unsalted butter
- 1 ½ cups corned beef, finely chopped, cooked
- Salt to taste
- ½ cup onion, chopped
- 1 ½ cups potatoes, chopped, cooked
- Pepper powder to taste
- A handful fresh parsley, chopped
- Eggs, to serve

Method:

1. Place a small cast iron skillet (preferably) over medium heat. Add butter. When butter melts, add onion and sauté until translucent.
2. Add potatoes and corned beef and stir. Spread the mixture all over the pan.
3. Raise the heat to medium high heat.
4. Using a metal spatula, press the mixture on to the bottom of the pan. Let it remain in this position without stirring for a while, until the underside is golden brown. If you find the mixture is getting stuck to the pan then add some more butter.
5. Flip sides and repeat the previous step.
6. Sprinkle parsley, salt and pepper and stir.
7. Cook eggs either sunny side up or poached.
8. Serve eggs with hash.

Traditional Irish Porridge

Serves: 4

Ingredients:

For porridge:

- ½ cup oatmeal
- 2 cups water
- A pinch salt

For topping: Optional, use as required

- Milk
- Dark chocolate nibs
- Honey
- Nuts of your choice

Method:

1. Add all the ingredients into a heavy bottomed pan. Place the pan over medium heat. Stir constantly with a wooden spatula.
2. When it begins to thicken, lower the heat and simmer for 12-15 minutes or until smooth and thick.
3. Ladle into bowls. Serve with any of the optional toppings if desired.

Irish Breakfast Porridge

Serves: 2

Ingredients:

- ½ cup steel cut oats
- ¼ teaspoon salt
- 2 cups water

For topping: Optional, use any, as required

- Butter
- Cream
- Fruit of your choice
- Maple syrup
- Any other topping of your choice

Method:

1. Add oats and water into a heavy bottomed pan. Place the pan over medium heat. Stir constantly with a wooden spatula.
2. When it begins to thicken, lower the heat and simmer for 12-15 minutes or until smooth and thick. Add salt and stir.
3. Ladle into bowls. Serve with any of the optional toppings if desired.

Irish Steel Cut Oatmeal

Serves: 2

Ingredients:

- ½ cup steel cut oats
- 2 cups water
- 1/8 teaspoon ground cinnamon
- 2-3 walnut halves or almonds or cashews, chopped
- Milk to serve (optional)
- 1 small banana, sliced
- Brown sugar or honey to taste

Method:

1. Pour water into a heavy bottom pan. Place the pan over medium heat.
2. When water begins to boil, add oats and cinnamon and stir constantly until it starts to become thick.
3. Reduce the heat and cook for 15-20 minutes. Stir occasionally. Do not overcook.
4. Turn off the heat. Add milk if using, brown sugar, banana and nuts and stir.
5. Ladle into bowls and serve.

Chapter Three: Traditional Irish Drinks Recipes

Original Irish Cream

Serves: 8

Ingredients:

- ¾ cup + 2 tablespoons Irish whiskey
- 7 ounces canned sweetened condensed milk
- ½ cup heavy cream
- ½ teaspoon instant coffee granules
- ½ teaspoon almond extract
- ½ teaspoon vanilla extract
- 1 tablespoon chocolate syrup

Method:

1. Add all the ingredients into a blender and blend until smooth.
2. Pour into a container with a fitting lid. Fasten the lid.
3. Chill until use.
4. Shake well before pouring into glasses.

Frozen Grasshopper

Serves: 4

Ingredients:

- 1 ½ ounces crème de menthe, green
- 4 cups vanilla ice cream
- A handful fresh mint leaves, to garnish
- 1 ½ ounce white crème de cacao
- 8 ice cubes

Method:

1. Add crème de menthe, vanilla, crème de cacao and ice cubes into a blender.
2. Blend for 30-40 seconds or until smooth.
3. Pour into glasses. Top with mint leaves and serve.

Lime Sherbet Punch

Serves: ½ punch bowl

Ingredients:

- 4 cups 7-Up soda
- ½ quart lime sherbet

Method:

1. Add 7 –Up into a punch bowl.
2. Scoop out lime sherbet and add into the bowl.
3. Serve.

Irish whiskey Maid with Jameson

Serves: 2

Ingredients:

- 4 ounces Jameson Black Barrel Whiskey
- 1.5 ounces simple syrup
- 4 fresh mint leaves to garnish
- 2 slices cucumber to garnish
- 6 slices Japanese cucumber, muddled
- 2 ounces lime juice

Method:

1. Add half the whiskey, half the simple syrup, half the lime juice and 3 slices Japanese cucumber into a shaker glass. Muddle with a muddler.
2. Add crushed ice. Fasten the lid and shake until well combined.
3. Pour into a glass. Place 2 mint leaves and a slice of cucumber in the glass and serve.
4. Repeat steps 1-2 to make the other serving.

Figs and Sage

Serves: 2

Ingredients:

- 1 ounce lemon juice
- 1.5 ounce East India sherry
- 2 fresh sage leaves
- 1 ounce fig syrup
- 3 ounces bourbon
- Bolivian pink salt to garnish

Method:

1. Add lemon juice, East India sherry, sage leaves, fig syrup and bourbon into a shaker.
2. Fasten the lid and shake until well combined.
3. Place crushed ice into 2 glasses. Strain the mixture into the glasses.
4. Sprinkle Bolivian pink salt on top and serve.

Kale St. Patrick's Day Cocktail

Serves: 2

Ingredients:

- 2 ounces kale juice
- 1 ounce cucumber juice
- ½ ounce simple syrup
- 3 ounces tequila Blanco
- 1.5 ounces ginger beer
- 1 ounce fresh lemon juice

Method:

1. Add kale juice, cucumber juice, simple syrup, tequila Blanco, ginger beer and lemon juice into a shaker.
2. Add ice. Fasten the lid and shake until well combined.
3. Pour into 2 glasses.
4. Sprinkle Bolivian pink salt on top and serve.

Saint Casa

Serves: 2

Ingredients:

- 3 ounces Casamigos Anejo
- ½ ounce agave nectar
- 1 ounce Crème de Mure
- Guinness beer to top off
- 4 fresh blackberries
- Edible gold and green glitter to sprinkle

Method:

1. Add Casamigos Anejo, agave nectar and Crème de Mure into a shaker.
2. Add ice. Fasten the lid and shake until well combined.
3. Pour into 2 glasses.
4. Top off with beer.
5. Take 2 toothpicks and fix 2 blackberries on each. Sprinkle edible gold and green glitter on top.
6. Garnish with a blackberry skewer in each glass and serve.

Irish Old Fashioned

Serves: 2

Ingredients:

- ½ ounce honey syrup (mix together 2 parts honey and 2 parts water and chill)
- 4 ounce Redbreast Irish whiskey
- 4 dashes Angostura bitters
- Lemon slices to garnish

Method:

1. Add all the ingredients into a jug and stir.
2. Add lots of ice and stir until well chilled. Let it sit for a while until it dilutes a little.
3. Place ice in 2 old fashioned glasses. Strain into the glasses.
4. Garnish with a lemon slice each and serve.

Matcha Honey Spritzer

Serves: 2

Ingredients:

- ½ teaspoon matcha powder
- 2 tablespoons honey
- 2 teaspoons warm water
- Ice as required
- 4 ounces ginger ale
- 6 ounces dry white wine
- Lemon wedges to garnish

Method:

1. Add matcha powder and warm water into the shaker and stir until matcha powder dissolves.
2. Add honey and stir until well combined.
3. Add ice, dry white wine and ginger ale.
4. Fasten the lid and shake until well combined.
5. Pour into 2 glasses.
6. Garnish with lemon slices and serve.

Irish Buck

Serves: 2

Ingredients:

- 4 ounces Irish whiskey
- 6 ounces ginger ale
- Ice, as required
- 2 tablespoons fresh lime juice
- Lime wedges to serve

Method:

1. Take 2 glasses and fill it up with crushed ice.
2. Stir in the whiskey, ginger ale and lime juice.
3. Garnish with lime wedges and serve.

Fuzzy Leprechaun Cocktail

Serves: 2

Ingredients:

- 2 ounces peach schnapps
- 2 ounces vodka
- 1 ounce pineapple juice
- 2 ounces blue Curacao
- 1 ounce orange juice
- Ice as required
- 2 cherries to garnish
- 2 orange slices to garnish

Method:

1. Add all the ingredients into a shaker and shake vigorously until well combined.
2. Pour into 2 glasses. Garnish with a cherry and an orange slice and serve.

Irish Sour Apple Cocktail

Serves: 2

Ingredients:

- 2 ounces Jameson Irish whiskey
- 7 ounces Fever-Tree Elderflower tonic water
- Ice cubes, as required
- 3 ounces Smirnoff Sour apple vodka
- Green apple slices

Method:

1. Add Whiskey, vodka and ice cubes into a shaker and stir for a few seconds.
2. Fill 2 glasses with ice.
3. Strain the whiskey mixture into the glasses. Discard the strained ice.
4. Add 3.5 ounces tonic water into each glass.
5. Decorate with apple slices and serve.

Irish Iced Coffee

Serves: 2

Ingredients:

- 4 ounces Tullamore Dew Irish whiskey
- 4 teaspoons Demerara sugar
- Whipped cream, to serve
- 2 teaspoons ground espresso
- 6 ounces cold brewed coffee
- 4 teaspoons hot water

Method:

1. Add whiskey and espresso into a small bowl. Stir and set aside for 15-20 minutes.
2. Place a coffee filter over a cocktail shaker. Pass the whisky mixture through it.
3. Add sugar and water into a bowl and stir until sugar dissolves completely.
4. Pour into the shaker. Also, pour cold brewed coffee. Add ice to fill the shaker. Fasten the lid.
5. Shake vigorously until well combined and the outside of the shaker looks frosted.
6. Add ice into 2 glasses. Pour the cocktail into the glasses.
7. Garnish with whipped cream and serve.

Chapter Four: Traditional Irish Side Dish Recipes

Simply Rich Cheddar Scalloped Potatoes

Serves: 3-4

Ingredients:

- 3 cups potatoes, peeled, thinly sliced
- 1 small onion, chopped
- 1 cup cheddar cheese, shredded
- Salt to taste
- Black pepper powder to taste
- 2 tablespoons margarine, cut into thin slices
- ¼ cup half and half
- 1 cup milk
- 2 tablespoons flour

Method:

1. Place a skillet over medium heat. Add margarine. When it melts, add onion and sauté until translucent.
2. Add flour, salt and pepper and stir for a few seconds.
3. Stir in the milk and half and half. Stir constantly until thick. Remove from heat. Add ¾ cup cheddar cheese and mix until well combined.
4. Add potatoes and mix well. Transfer into a casserole dish. Cover the dish with foil.
5. Bake in a preheated oven at 350° F for about 30 -40 minutes or until the potatoes are tender. Uncover and top with ¼ cup cheese or+ use more if you like it cheesy. Bake until the edges are light brown.

Irish Mushy Peas

Serves: 2-3

Ingredients:

- 4 ounces dried split marrowfat peas
- 1 ¾ cups boiling water
- Pepper powder to taste
- Butter, as required
- ¼ teaspoon baking soda
- Salt to taste
- A pinch sugar

Method:

1. Add peas into a bowl. Pour water over the peas. Add baking soda and stir. Let it soak for 7-8 hours.
2. Drain and add into a pot. Cover with water and place pot over medium heat.
3. When it begins to boil, lower the heat and cook until soft. When soft, drain the excess water.
4. Add salt, pepper, butter and sugar and stir. Mash lightly and serve.

Scalloped Cabbage

Serves: 3

Ingredients:

- 1 medium head cabbage, cut into
- Salt to taste
- 6 tablespoons milk
- ¼ cup + 2 tablespoons margarine
- ½ package club crackers, crushed
- ½ cup cold water
- 4 teaspoons flour
- Pepper powder to taste
- ¼ pound Velveeta cheese

Method:

1. Place cabbage in a bowl. Add a little salt and stir.
2. Add cold water.
3. Place a skillet over medium heat. Add ¼ cup margarine. When it melts, stir in the flour and whisk for 10-15 seconds.
4. Pour milk and stir constantly until thick. Stir in the cheese. Cook until it melts.
5. Place cabbage in a baking dish. Season with salt and pepper. Spread the cheese sauce over the cabbage.
6. Add cracker into a bowl. Melt 2 tablespoons margarine and add into the bowl. Mix well.
7. Sprinkle the crackers over the sauce.
8. Bake in a preheated oven at 350° F for about 30 -40 minutes or until golden brown on top.

Chapter Five: Traditional Irish Appetizer Recipes

Smoked Salmon on Irish Soda Bread Crostini

Serves: 3

Ingredients:

- 6 slices Irish soda bread, toasted
- ¼ cup butter
- 4 ounces smoked salmon
- ½ tablespoon chives, chopped
- 1 teaspoon fresh dill, chopped, to garnish

Method:

1. Add butter and chives into a bowl and stir.
2. Spread the mixture on one side of each slice of bread.
3. Spread salmon over each. Garnish with dill.
4. Cut into desired shape and serve.

St. Patrick's Day Deviled Eggs

Serves: 6

Ingredients:

- 6 eggs
- 2 tablespoons mayonnaise
- 4 drops green food coloring
- Green egg dye
- 1 small stalk celery from heart, minced
- 12 small parsley leaves

Method:

1. Add eggs into a saucepan. Cover with water. Place the saucepan over medium heat.
2. When it begins to boil, turn off the heat. Let the eggs remain in the saucepan for 15 minutes.
3. Drain the water and add cold water into the bowl. Place the bowl in the refrigerator for 30 minutes.
4. Make the egg dye following the instructions on the package. Carefully crack the eggs but do not peel. Each egg should be cracked at different spots so that the dye can get in through the cracks.
5. Now dip the eggs in the green dye for about 5 minutes.
6. Rinse and peel the eggs now. Cut into 2 halves lengthwise.
7. Carefully remove the egg yolks and place in a bowl. Mash the yolks and add celery, mayonnaise and green food coloring.
8. Fill the yolk mixture in the cavity of the eggs.
9. Garnish each half with a leaf of parsley and serve.

Cheese Dip

Serves: 5

Ingredients:

- ¾ cup Irish cheddar cheese, shredded
- ¼ cup green onion, finely chopped
- 1 teaspoon prepared horseradish
- ½ cup plain yogurt
- 2 tablespoons mayonnaise
- ½ teaspoon ground pepper

Method:

1. Add all the ingredients into a bowl and mix well. Chill and serve.

Pistachio Twists

Serves: 20

Ingredients:

- ½ package (from a 17.5 ounces package) frozen puff pastry sheets, thawed
- ¼ cup pistachio nuts, finely chopped
- 4 egg yolks
- 2/3 cup sugar
- 2 tablespoons water
- 4 tablespoons butter or margarine, melted
- 1 teaspoon ground cardamom
- 1 teaspoon ground cinnamon
- Flour, to dust

Method:

1. Place a sheet of parchment paper on a baking sheet. Use 2 baking sheets if desired.
2. Beat together yolk and water in a small bowl.
3. Dust your countertop with a little flour. Place a sheet of puff pastry over it and roll each until it is a square for about 9 inches. Take another sheet and repeat the same process.
4. Brush the sheets with egg yolk mixture. Sprinkle half the sugar over the sheets. Sprinkle half the pistachio nuts on one sheet. Do not sprinkle sugar or pistachio nuts along the border of the pastry sheets (about ¼ inch).
5. Cover the sheet (with pistachio) with the other sheet (that has only sugar on it), the sugar side facing down. Press the edges to seal.
6. Brush 2 tablespoons melted butter on top of the pastry. Cut into strips of about ¾ inch width.

41

7. Take a pistachio strip and twist it thrice. Repeat with all the strips. Place on the prepared baking sheet. Leave a gap of 2 inches between 2 twists.
8. Repeat steps 3-7 with the remaining 2 puff pastry sheets.
9. Bake in a preheated oven at 350° F for about 20 minutes or until golden brown on top.
10. Remove the baking sheet from the oven immediately and place on a wire rack to cool completely. Serve.
11. Store leftovers in an airtight container.
12. To serve: Reheat in an oven for 5 minutes and serve.

Avocado Bacon Pinwheels

Serves: 12-15

Ingredients:

- 4 ripe avocadoes, mashed
- 4 tablespoons lime juice
- 1 cup cilantro, chopped
- Salt and pepper to taste
- 6 tablespoons Greek yogurt
- 4 cups cooked chicken, diced
- 1 cup bacon, chopped
- 4 cups Kerrygold Aged cheddar cheese, shredded
- 12 tortillas (8 inches each)

Method:

1. Spread the tortillas on your countertop.
2. Mix together rest of the ingredients and spread over the tortillas. Roll the tortillas tightly. Place on a tray, with its seam side facing down. Refrigerate for an hour.
3. Chop into ¼ inch thick slices and serve.

Chapter Six: Irish Lunch Recipes

Irish Zucchini and Potato Pancakes

Serves: 12

Ingredients:

- 2 cups prepared mashed potatoes
- ½ cup milk
- 6 tablespoons unsalted butter
- 3 cups Yukon gold potatoes, shredded
- 2 small zucchinis, shredded
- 2 cups all-purpose flour
- 2 eggs
- 3-4 teaspoons fine sea salt or to taste
- 2 cups cheddar cheese, shredded
- Canola oil to make pancakes, as required

Method:

1. Add mashed potatoes, milk, salt, flour, eggs and butter into a bowl and whisk well.
2. Stir in the shredded potatoes, zucchini and cheddar cheese and mix well.
3. Place a large nonstick pan or griddle over medium heat. When the pan is heated, add 1-2 tablespoons oil. When oil is heated, place about 2 tablespoons of the potato mixture on the pan. Spread it until it is ¼ inch thick. You can make 2-3 more pancakes simultaneously.

4. Cook until the underside is golden brown. Flip sides and cook the other side too.
5. Remove and place on a baking sheet. Place the baking sheet in the oven to keep warm.
6. Repeat the above 3 steps and make the remaining pancakes.

Irish Pub Salad

Serves: 4

Ingredients:

- 1 cup mayonnaise
- 4 teaspoons fresh tarragon, chopped or 1 ½ teaspoons dried tarragon
- 5-6 teaspoons water
- 1 cup pickled beets, chopped
- 1 cucumber, sliced
- 2 tomatoes, chopped
- 1 cup celery, chopped
- 1 cup onion, sliced
- 3 cups cabbage, shredded
- 8 cups torn Boston lettuce or Bibb lettuce
- 8 ounces cheddar cheese or blue cheese, cut into wedges
- 4 hardboiled eggs, peeled, chopped
- 4 tablespoons malt vinegar or white wine vinegar
- 2 teaspoons whole grain Dijon mustard
- Salt to taste
- Pepper powder to taste

Method:

1. Add mayonnaise, tarragon, vinegar and Dijon mustard into a bowl. Mix until well combined.
2. Add water, salt and pepper and mix well. The dressing should be of dropping consistency.
3. Spread the lettuce leaves on a large serving platter.
4. Place rest of the vegetables in whatever manner you like to decorate, over the lettuce.
5. Place egg slices right on top. Pour the dressing all over the salad.

6. Scatter the cheese wedges and serve.

Irish Flag Salad

Serves: 2

Ingredients:

For salad:

- 3 ounces fresh baby spinach
- 1 medium orange, peeled, separated into segments, deseeded
- 1 tablespoon pistachio nuts, chopped
- 1 medium pear, thinly sliced
- 1 tablespoon crumbled feta cheese

For dressing:

- 1 ½ tablespoons canola oil
- 2 teaspoons lemon juice
- ¼ teaspoon orange zest, grated
- 1 tablespoon orange juice
- ½ teaspoon honey
- Salt to taste

Method:

1. Spread the spinach equally between 2 plates.
2. Divide and place pear slices, orange, cheese and pistachio over the spinach.
3. Add all the ingredients of dressing into a bowl and whisk well.
4. Pour over the salad.
5. Serve.

Green Salad

Serves: 2

Ingredients:

For salad:

- 3 cups greens of your choice (you can use a mixture of greens if desired)
- 6-8 spears asparagus, trimmed or asparagus tips, trimmed
- 1 ounce Irish cheddar cheese, chopped into small pieces
- 1 large green bell pepper, chopped
- 1 small Granny Smith apple, cored, chopped, tossed with a little lemon juice
- 1 tablespoon mint leaves, minced
- ½ small parsnip or ½ small carrot, grated
- 2 tablespoons raisins

For dressing:

- ¼ cup whole milk buttermilk
- 1-2 tablespoons apple cider vinegar
- Salt to taste
- A little cream for thinning (optional)
- 1 tablespoon sour cream of plain yogurt
- Pepper powder to taste

Method:

1. To make dressing: Add all the ingredients of dressing into a bowl and whisk well.
2. Add greens asparagus, cheddar cheese, apple, bell pepper, mint leaves and parsnips into a bowl and toss well.

3. Divide into 2 plates. Sprinkle raisins on top. Drizzle the dressing over it and serve.

Irish Dubliner Salad

Serves:

Ingredients:

- 2 heads butter lettuce, rinsed, spun dried, coarsely chopped
- 10-12 ounces Irish Dubliner cheese, grated
- 2 carrots, thinly sliced or grated
- A handful fresh herbs of your choice, minced
- 16 ounces pickled red beets, grated or raw beets, grated
- 1 ½ cups English cucumber, thinly sliced
- 2 cups red cabbage, shredded

For vinaigrette:

- 2/3-cup salad oil (sunflower, grape seed, safflower, etc.)
- 6 tablespoons white vinegar
- 4 teaspoons Irish mustard
- Salt to taste
- Pepper powder to taste

Method:

1. To make vinaigrette: Add all the ingredients of vinaigrette into a bowl and whisk well. Cover and set aside for a while.
2. Place lettuce leaves in a large, shallow bowl.
3. Place rest of the salad ingredients over the lettuce in any manner you desire.
4. Pour dressing on top and serve.

Saint Paddy's Irish Sandwich

Serves: 3

Ingredients:

- 1 ½ pounds corned beef brisket with spice packet
- ½ tablespoon balsamic vinegar
- ¼ teaspoon salt
- 1 small head cabbage, cored, thinly sliced
- 6 slices sourdough bread, lightly toasted
- 1 tablespoon olive oil
- ½ tablespoon spicy brown mustard + extra to spread on the bread slices
- Pepper powder to taste

Method:

1. Add corned beef into a pot. Pour enough water to cover. Stir in the spice packet. Cover with lid.
2. When it begins to boil, lower the heat and simmer until tender. It should take 50 minutes for every pound of meat to cook. Remove meat from the pot and place on your cutting board. Discard the water in the pot.
3. When cool enough to handle, cut into slices across the grain.
4. Add oil, mustard, vinegar, pepper and salt into a bowl and whisk well.
5. Add cabbage and toss well.
6. Spread mustard on 3 of the bread slices. Top with cabbage and corned beef. Cover with the remaining 3 bread slices.
7. Cut into desired shape and serve.

Leftover Corned Beef Sandwich

Serves: 4

Ingredients:

- 4 small ciabatta, halved, horizontally
- 4 ounces provolone cheese, deli sliced
- 12 ounces leftover corned beef

Method:

1. Place corned beef on the bottom halves of the ciabatta.
2. Place cheese slices over it.
3. Place in the toaster oven and heat for a few minutes until cheese melts.
4. Cover sandwiches with the top half of ciabatta and bake for a few minutes until the sandwiches are warm.
5. Cut into desired shape and serve.

Irish Potato and Leek Soup

Serves: 8-10

Ingredients:

- 4 teaspoons vegetable oil
- 4 stalks celery, chopped
- 4 cloves garlic, minced
- 8 cups vegetable stock or water
- 1 teaspoon pepper powder
- 3 cups light cream
- 4 teaspoons fresh dill, chopped
- 4 teaspoons fresh parsley, chopped
- 4 teaspoons fresh tarragon, chopped
- 4 cups leeks, chopped
- 2 small onions, chopped
- 8 medium potatoes, peeled, coarsely chopped
- 2 teaspoons salt
- 1 teaspoon dried thyme

Method:

1. Place a soup pot over medium heat. Add oil. When the oil is heated, add leeks, onion, celery and garlic and sauté until soft.
2. Add stock, thyme, salt, pepper and potatoes. When it begins to boil, lower the heat and simmer until potatoes are tender.
3. Stir in the cream and all the fresh herbs. Stir occasionally. Let it simmer for a few minutes. Turn off the heat. Set aside for 10 minutes.
4. Ladle into soup bowls and serve with warm bread.

Chapter Seven: Traditional Irish Main Course Recipes

Colcannon Soup

Serves: 3

- ¾ pound boiling potatoes, peeled, cut into 1 inch cubes
- 1 cup cabbage, shredded
- ½ pound leeks, white and pale green parts only, chopped
- 2 ½ cups chicken stock
- Salt to taste
- White pepper powder to taste
- 2 tablespoons butter
- ½ cup + 2 tablespoons half and half
- A pinch ground nutmeg
- A handful parsley, chopped

Method:

1. Place a large saucepan over medium heat. Add butter. When butter melts, add cabbage, leeks and potatoes. Sauté for a minute. Cover with a lid and cook until just tender. Add stock and stir.
2. When the stock begins to boil, lower the heat and cover with a lid. Cook until soft.
3. Add salt, pepper and nutmeg. Stir until well combined. Turn off the heat. Cool for a while.

4. Transfer into a food processor and blend until smooth or blend with an immersion blender.
5. Pour it back into the saucepan. Heat thoroughly. Add half and half and stir.
6. Ladle into soup bowls and serve.

Irish Roasted Salmon

Serves: 2

Ingredients:

- 1 tablespoon honey
- 2 tablespoons Irish whiskey
- ¾ teaspoon lemon zest, grated
- Salt to taste
- Freshly ground pepper to taste
- 2 tablespoons cider vinegar
- 1 teaspoon fresh thyme
- 1 tablespoon vegetable oil
- 2 salmon fillets

Method:

1. Place salmon in a bowl. Add rest of the ingredients into another bowl and stir. Pour into the bowl of salmon. Marinate for 4-5 hours in the refrigerator.
2. Place a rack in the roasting pan. Place roasting pan in the oven.
3. Pull out the salmon from the bowl and place on the rack.
4. Bake in a preheated oven at 350° F for about 10-12 minutes. Baste once with the marinade.
5. Bake until golden brown and cooked through.

Irish Lasagna

Serves: 3-4

Ingredients:

- ½ pound real Irish minced beef
- 1 small egg, beaten
- ½ teaspoon mixture of dried basil, thyme and oregano
- 4 ounces mozzarella cheese, shredded
- 6 lasagna sheets
- ½ pint ricotta cheese
- 1 clove garlic, crushed
- 4 ounces spaghetti squash
- 6 tablespoons parmesan cheese

Method:

1. Place a skillet over medium heat. Add beef. Sauté until brown. Drain excess fat and set aside the meat.
2. Add ricotta, herbs, egg and half the mozzarella cheese into a bowl and mix well.
3. Spread a little spaghetti sauce on the bottom of a baking dish.
4. Place 2 lasagna sheets over it.
5. Spread 1/3 of the cheese mixture followed by 1/3 of the beef mixture.
6. Spread some spaghetti sauce over it.
7. Repeat steps 4-6 twice.
8. Sprinkle Parmesan cheese and remaining mozzarella cheese.
9. Cover the dish with foil.
10. Bake in a preheated oven at 350° F for about 30 minutes. Uncover and bake until top is brown.
11. Serve hot.

Stuffed Cabbage Rolls

Serves: 3

Ingredients:

- 1 medium head cabbage, cored
- 1 medium onion, chopped
- 2 ounces pork sausage
- ¼ teaspoon allspice
- 4 ounces canned tomato sauce
- ½ teaspoon salt
- ½ teaspoon dried thyme
- ½ tablespoon butter
- 6 ounces lean ground beef
- ½ cup white rice or ½ cup brown rice, cooked
- 14 ounces canned tomatoes, with its juice
- 3 ounces canned tomato paste
- ¼ teaspoon garlic salt
- Sour cream, as required

Method:

1. Place a pot with water over medium heat. Add the whole cabbage into it. Let it cook until slightly soft. (Soft enough for you to be able to separate the leaves). Drain the water.
2. When cool enough to handle, separate the leaves. Shake to drop off any water droplets. Set aside.
3. Place a skillet over medium heat. Add butter. When butter melts, add onions and sauté until golden brown.
4. Add half the sautéed onions into a bowl. Also add rice, allspice, beef and pork sausage.
5. Using your hands mix well.

6. Place the skillet with half the onions back over low heat. Add tomato paste, tomato sauce, tomatoes, salt, pepper, garlic salt and thyme and stir. Let it cook for 10-12 minutes. Turn off the heat.
7. Spread the cabbage leaves on your countertop. Place a little of the filling near the stem side. Roll the cabbage and place with its seam side facing down in a baking dish that is greased with a little butter.
8. Repeat with all the filling and leaves.
9. Pour the cooked sauce over the rolls.
10. Bake in a preheated oven at 350° F for about 50-60 minutes.
11. Drizzle sour cream on top and serve.

Irish Stout Chicken

Serves: 2-3

Ingredients:

- 1 tablespoon vegetable oil
- 1 large clove garlic, minced
- 3 carrots, peeled, chopped
- 1 small onion, chopped
- 2 pounds chicken, cut into pieces
- 1 parsnip, peeled, chopped
- Salt to taste
- Pepper to taste
- ½ teaspoon dried thyme
- 1/3 – ½ cup stout beer
- 1/3 cup frozen peas
- ¼ pound button mushrooms

Method:

1. Place a skillet over medium heat. Add oil. When the oil is heated, add onion and garlic and sauté until translucent.
2. Remove with a slotted spoon and place in a bowl.
3. Place the chicken pieces in the skillet, in a single layer. Cover with a lid. Cook until light brown on all the sides.
4. Add the cooked onions back into the skillet. Add parsnip, carrot, salt, pepper and thyme and stir.
5. Pour beer over the chicken. When it begins to boil, lower the heat and cover with a lid.
6. Simmer until chicken is cooked through.
7. Remove the lid and cook on high heat for a few minutes until the sauce is thickened.

Bacon and Cabbage Pies

Serves: 3

Ingredients:

- 3 tablespoons butter
- 1 carrot, peeled, finely chopped
- 1 medium onion, thinly sliced
- ½ head green cabbage, chopped
- ¾ cup hot chicken stock
- ¾ teaspoon English mustard
- 1 tablespoon plain flour + extra to dust
- Salt to taste
- Freshly ground pepper to taste
- 1/3 cup single cream
- 6 ounces frozen short crust pastry, thawed
- 1 pound bacon joint
- 1 small egg yolk

Method:

1. Place bacon in a pot. Cover with cold water. Place the pot over medium heat.
2. When it begins to boil, lower the heat and simmer until cooked through. Remove the bacon and set aside on a plate. Retain a little of the stock (about ½ cup) and discard the rest.
3. Place a pan over medium heat. Add 1-tablespoon butter. When butter melts, add onion and carrot and sauté until golden brown. Turn off the heat.
4. Place a saucepan over medium heat. Add remaining butter. When butter melts, add flour and stir constantly for about a minute.
5. Pour slowly the bacon stock stirring constantly until it thickens.

6. Lower the heat and let it cook for 2-3 minutes.
7. Add cream, salt, mustard and pepper and stir. Add bacon and cabbage and mix well. Turn off the heat.
8. Dust your countertop with flour. Place the pastry on the countertop and roll with a rolling pin. Make 3 rounds from the rolled pastry to line a mini pie pan and make 3 smaller rounds to cover the pies.
9. Place the bigger rounds in the mini pie pans. Place a little of the filling in each pan. Brush egg on the edges of the pastry. Cover with the smaller rounds.
10. Press the edges of both the rounds together to seal. Brush the top of the crust with egg.
11. Bake in a preheated oven at 350° F until the crust is golden brown.
12. Remove from the oven and cool for a few minutes before serving.

Vegetable Shepherd's Pie

Serves: 5-6

Ingredients:

For topping:

- 1 ½ pounds Yukon gold potatoes, with skin
- 1 ½ pounds russet potatoes, with skin
- Kosher salt to taste

For filling:

- ½ ounce dried porcini mushrooms
- 3 cloves garlic cloves
- 1 tablespoon garlic, chopped
- 2 ½ tablespoons olive oil, divided
- 1 tablespoon tomato paste
- 1 cup dry white wine
- 1 tablespoon cornstarch
- Freshly ground pepper to taste
- ½ cup frozen pearl onions, thawed, halved
- 1 cup mixed fresh mushrooms, chopped into bite size pieces
- 6 tablespoons brown or French green lentils
- ½ teaspoon kosher salt + extra to season
- 1 ½ cups onion, chopped
- 1 bay leaf
- 4 cups vegetable broth
- 1 tablespoon gluten free white miso or tamari soy sauce
- 6 cups mixed fall vegetables like carrot, squash, parsnip, etc.
- 1 sprig rosemary
- A handful mixed fresh herbs of your choice.

Method:

1. To make topping: Place a sheet of foil on a baking sheet. Place all the potatoes on the baking sheet.
2. Bake in a preheated oven at 450° F until cooked through. It may take 45-60 minutes.
3. Place the potatoes into a ricer and rice the potatoes. Place in a large bowl. Add butter and mix well.
4. Add milk and salt and stir. Cover and set aside.
5. To make filling: Place porcini in a bowl. Pour 1-2 cups hot water over it. Set aside for a while.
6. Meanwhile, make the lentils as follows: Add lentils, 1 clove garlic, 2 cups water and salt into a saucepan. Place the saucepan over medium heat.
7. When it begins to boil, lower the heat and simmer until soft. Do not overcook.
8. Drain excess water in the lentils and throw away the garlic clove.
9. To make sauce: Place a heavy pot over medium heat. Add 1-½ tablespoons of oil. When the oil is heated, add onions and sauté until light brown. Stir in the chopped garlic and sauté until fragrant.
10. Add tomato paste and cook for a couple of minutes.
11. Stir in the bay leaf and wine. Scrape the bottom of the pan to remove any browned bits that may be stuck. Add porcini into the pan along with the soaked water. Do not add any residue of the mushrooms.
12. Cook until the liquid in the pot is half its original quantity. Add broth and stir. Cook until the broth is half its original quantity.
13. Pass the mixture through a strainer into a saucepan. Place the saucepan over medium heat. When the mixture begins to boil, mix together a little water and

cornstarch and add into the saucepan. Stir constantly until thick.

14. Add miso, salt and pepper and mix well.
15. Add vegetables, 2 cloves garlic, rosemary sprig and pearl onions into a bowl. Drizzle 1-tablespoon oil. Toss well. Transfer on to a rimmed baking sheet.
16. Bake in a preheated oven at 450° F until cooked through. Transfer into a bowl and add fresh mushrooms. Toss well.
17. Mash the garlic cloves and add into the cooked sauce. Throw off the rosemary sprig.
18. To assemble: Spread the lentils in a baking dish. Spread the vegetables over the lentils. Spread sauce over the vegetables. Top with potato mixture.
19. Bake in a preheated oven at 450° F until top is brown.
20. Remove from the oven. Cool for a few minutes and serve.

Chapter Eight: Traditional Irish Dessert Recipes

St. Patrick's Day Parfaits

Serves: 8

Ingredients:

- 2 boxes (3 ounces each, 4 servings each) Jell-O instant pistachio pudding mix
- 4 kiwifruits, peeled, thinly sliced
- 6 drops green food coloring
- 4 cups milk
- Cool whip, as required
- Green coarse sugar, to garnish

Method:

1. Make the pudding following the instructions on the package with milk. Place in the refrigerator until it sets.
2. Add green drops into the bowl of cool whip and stir.
3. Take 8 parfait glasses. Layer the pudding, cool whip and rest of the ingredients in the glasses in any manner you desire.
4. Garnish with green sugar and chill until use.

St. Patrick's Day Crispy Treats

Serves: 12

Ingredients:

- 3 cups Rice Krispies
- ¼ teaspoon vanilla extract
- 5 ounces mini marshmallows
- 2 tablespoons margarine
- Green food coloring, as required
- Gold chocolate coins, to garnish

Method:

1. Grease a baking dish with a little oil or butter.
2. Place a pan over low heat. Add margarine. When it melts, stir in the marshmallows. Keep stirring until the marshmallows are completely melted. Turn off the heat.
3. Stir in vanilla and food coloring.
4. Add rice Krispies into the pan and stir quickly until well combined.
5. Transfer into the prepared baking dish. Press it evenly on to the bottom of the baking pan using a spatula that is greased with a little butter. Let it cool completely.
6. Slice into bars. Top with gold chocolate coins on each bar and serve.

Chocolate Mint Candy (Fudge)

Serves: About 30-35

Ingredients:

- 6 ounces semi-sweet chocolate chips
- 1 teaspoon vanilla extract
- 1-2 teaspoons peppermint extract
- 7 ounces canned sweetened condensed milk, divided
- 3 ounces white candy coating
- 6 drops green food coloring

Method:

1. Place a heavy saucepan over medium heat. Add chocolate chips and ½ cup condensed milk. When the chocolate melts, turn off the heat. Stir frequently.
2. Add vanilla and mix well.
3. Line a small square pan with wax paper. Spread half the mixture into the pan. Place the pan in the refrigerator for 10 minutes or until set.
4. Meanwhile, place a saucepan over low heat. Add candy coating and remaining condensed milk and stir until the candy coating melts and the mixture is creamy.
5. Add green color and peppermint extract and stir until well combined.
6. Pour over the firm chocolate layer in the pan. Place in the refrigerator for a few hours until it sets.
7. Chop into 1 inch squares and serve.

Kiwifruit Lime Jell-O with Yogurt

Serves: 8

Ingredients:

- 2 packages lime Jell-O
- 4 cups ice cubes
- ½ cup plain yogurt + extra to garnish
- 2 cups kiwifruits, halved, thinly sliced
- 8 slices kiwifruit to garnish
- 2 cups boiling water

Method:

1. Add Jell-O powder into a bowl. Pour boiling water into it. Mix until well combined and dissolved completely.
2. Stir in the ice cubes. Keep stirring until it thickens. Discard any ice cubes that are remaining in the bowl.
3. Set aside 1 cup of the Jell-O in the refrigerator for 30 minutes. After 30 minutes add yogurt and stir. Beat on high speed until it is twice the original quantity.
4. Place the remaining Jell-O also in the refrigerator until it thickens slightly.
5. Add kiwifruits into this bowl and fold gently. Refrigerate until set.
6. Spoon into glasses.
7. Garnish with yogurt and a slice of kiwi and serve.

Conclusion

Thank you once again for choosing the book.

This book brings Ireland's rich culinary heritage to life. Most traditional Irish recipes are difficult to make since there is a lot of technique involved. It takes time for someone, even from Ireland, to master those techniques. But, this does not mean that you cannot make those dishes at home.

Over the course of the book, you will have learned how to make different traditional recipes easily. Follow the directions written under each recipe, and at the end of the process, you can serve a complete Irish traditional meal and surprise your friends and family.

I hope you enjoy the recipes mentioned in this book.

Finally, if you enjoyed this book, then I'd like to ask you for a favor. Will you be kind enough to leave a review for this book on Amazon? It would be greatly appreciated!

Thank you and good luck!

Other Books by Grizzly Publishing

"Jamaican Cookbook: Traditional Jamaican Recipes Made Easy"

https://www.amazon.com/dp/B07B68KL8D

"Brazilian Instant Pot Cookbook: Delicious Pressure Cooked Meals Made Fast and Easy"

https://www.amazon.com/dp/B078XBYP89

"Norwegian Cookbook: Traditional Scandinavian Recipes Made Easy"

https://www.amazon.com/dp/B079M2W223

"Casserole Cookbook: Delicious Casserole Recipes From Around The World"

https://www.amazon.com/dp/B07B6GV61Q

Printed in the USA
CPSIA information can be obtained
at www.ICGtesting.com
LVHW021427131023
761031LV00005B/61

9 781952 395451